DOGS

Written and illustrated by

MARK BARDSLEY

Text and illustrations © Mark Bardsley 2019
The moral right of the author has been asserted

First published in 2019 by Mark Bardsley
www.markbardsleyillustration.co.uk

ABOUT THE AUTHOR

Mark Bardsley was born in 1963 in Essex, England and spent most of his childhood in a crumbling Shropshire manor house with his eccentric family and an exotic menagerie of animals. They included a disinterested Pony called Misty, a bumbly Boxer named Simon, a knotty Afghan Hound called Samantha and a very loud Peacock called Sylvester (the world's most reliable alarm clock!)

Mark has been a freelance artist for many years but has also taught art, constructed strange musical instruments and managed a community theatre. His illustrations have appeared on British television including BBC 2's Autumn Watch series. He is passionate about the natural world!

This is his second illustrated book about animals.
Mark Bardsley's Crazy Pet Poems is also available.

Dedicated to the memory of
Long Lost Friends

Simon & Samantha, Whisky & Mac,
Dylan & Kelly, Flexi & Scamp, Mitsy & Chloe, Blossom, Cassie,
Claudius, Matt, Benjamin, Oscar, Pedro, Candy & Amy.

Introduction

Dogs and the relationship we have with them is a subject that has long fascinated me. We seem to imaginatively superimpose our own foibles upon them while all they really want to do is live their lives like the wolves in dogs clothing that they are. Dogs are forever reminding us that it is animal kind that has to put up with us and not the other way round.

Over thousands of years we have managed to distort them into an astonishing variety of shapes and sizes to suit all the jobs we have foisted upon them. Since the dawn of civilisation they have sat on thrones with us, herded and hunted for us, guided those with impairments, gone to war, soothed our troubled hearts and been blasted into space! Rightly or wrongly we have embroiled them in human existence and they have become deeply embedded in our culture.

The 1960s saw dogs taking centre stage in the media driven era of 'flower power'. The Rolling Stones, Marianne Faithful, Jeff Beck and Salvador Dali were all accompanied by Afghan hounds. The Beatles were photographed hugging their dogs and Paul McCartney's Old English Sheep Dog Martha was the subject of 'Martha my dear', a track from the Beatles White Album of 1968.

It was not perhaps totally without coincidence then, that my parents became the proud owners of Samantha the Afghan Hound in 1965 and my trendy Uncle Dennis lumbered himself with an out-of-control Old English Sheep Dog called Benjamin, who while not meaning anyone any harm could send a crowd running for cover! Two of the poems in this collection are inspired by these old friends.

To the cartoonist the dog family is a gift, largely thanks to human intervention and, let's face it, in some instances our creativity has somewhat overstepped the bounds of nature, giving rise to creatures of legendary countenance. Through the mediums of literature and television we have expanded even this.

Indeed, as a child in the sixties my television-enhanced dream world was inhabited by the likes of Scooby, Snoopy, Droopy, Goofy, Basil, Butch, Fleegle, Hector, Sweep, Spotty, Lassie, Muttley, Hong Kong Fooey, Mungo, Huckleberry and Dougal to name a few.

The BBC's Blue Peter programme was in its infancy then and drew huge audiences of junior dog lovers by buddying up presenters with a Blue Peter dog. There have been ten Blue Peter dogs to date.
My first ever serious attempts at illustrating dogs were featured on the drawing of Peter Purves, John Noakes and Valerie Singleton that I sent to the BBC television Centre in 1973 aged ten. To my great delight I was awarded the customary Blue Peter badge.

But most charming of all was Cécile Aubry's 1965 hit children's series, 'Belle and Sebastian' set in the breathtaking snow covered French Alps. It told the story of six year old orphan Sebastian, played by Aubry's son, and Belle an enormous and heart-meltingly cuddly looking Pyrenean Mountain Dog (every dog loving kid's dream). Such is the nostalgic power of this production in retrospect, that its haunting theme tune alone is enough to make me feel like a wide-eyed five year old again! My Pyrenean Mountain Dog illustration in this collection is my tribute to this wonderfully evocative production!

Ten of the fifty-one poems presented here are inspired by real dogs I have known and this book is dedicated to their memory.
Sigmund Freud's Chow Chow, Jofi is referenced. She became a helpful feature of his therapy sessions. Freud considered her presence in his treatment room to be calming for his patients. Thankfully, therapy and assistance dogs are now becoming more widely available.

Many of my illustrations have been influenced by dogs I have met when drawing at live events. I hope some of them remind you of dogs who in making your acquaintance have touched, enlightened and entertained you.

Mark Bardsley June 2019

CONTENTS

8. A Number of Clumbers *(Clumber Spaniel)*
10. A Proper Charlie *(Cavalier King Charles Spaniel)*
12. A Spaniel in the Works *(Springer Spaniel)*
14. Afghan Hound
16. Aimless Amy *(Cocker Spaniel)*
18. Alsatian at the Station
20. Bedlington
22. Beware Dale of the Airdale!
24. Bichon Frise
26. Bingo the Dingo
28. Borzoi Ballet
30. Chinese Crested Powder Puff
32. Chow Chow
34. Cockerpoo
36. Comedy Duo *(Boxer and Bulldog)*
38. Dalmation Contemplation
40. Dandy Dinmont
42. Dido *(Great Dane)*
44. Don't upset my Setter! *(Irish Setter)*
46. French Bulldog
48. Gypsy *(Jack Russell)*
50. Husky
52. Jack *(Lancashire Heeler)*
54. Komondor
56. Labrador
58. Lady Chihuahua
60. Manchester Terrier
62. Mexican Hairless
64. My Pug has a Bug
66. Neopolitan Mastiff
68. Ode to Mongrels
70. Old English Sheep Dog
72. Oscar the Beagle
74. Pedro *(Rough Collie)*

76. Pointless *(Pointer)*
78. Puggle
80. Pyrenean Mountain Dog *(and Yorkshire Terrier)*
82. Retriever Believer *(Golden Retriever)*
84. Saint Bernard
86. Saluki
88. Samoyed
90. Schnauzer
92. Shar Pei
94. Shih Tzu
96. Staffie
98. The Royal Corgis
100. The Skye Terrier Song
102. Thieving Hound *(Griffon Fauve de Bretagne)*
104. Westie Bestie
106. Whippet
108. Wolfman

A Number of Clumbers

A number of Clumbers
May well be a clumble?
A clumsy, a crumble,
Perhaps just a jumble?
Or maybe it's known as a
Rumble and tumble,
A whimsy, a whumble,
A gimble, a gumble.

A foible, a fumble,
A shambles, a gambol,
A gremble, a gramble,
A brimble a bramble.

Nobody knows what to call
Such a tangle,
But one day I'll come up
With just the right angle.

A Proper Charlie

Auntie's Spaniel Bing
Thought that he was king;
A proper Charlie,
Rather rude –
A cavalier attitude!

A Spaniel in the Works

When you get knocked off your feet
Or there's been a theft of meat,
When the floor's not looking neat
Or there's chickens in the street,
          There's a Spaniel in the works!

When the cat is looking glum
And the house is like a slum,
When you holler, 'Look out Mum!'
And your Nan lands on her bum,
          There's a Spaniel in the works!

When your coat is torn to shreds
And things disappear from sheds,
When the veggie beds look dead
And every stem has lost its head,
          There's a Spaniel in the works!

When the bees have been molested
And the neighbourhood infested,
When their patience has been tested
And your family arrested,
          There's a Spaniel in the works!

When the year has fully turned
And your town is trashed and burned,
When by all you have been spurned
You will certainly have learned,
          There's a Spaniel in the works!

Zoom

Afghan Hound

Afghan hound
Basket-bound
Nose and hair
Legs in the air.

An unfamiliar
Distant sound?
Now she is up
Horizon found.

She points
Her supersonic beak
A blur of fur
She's at her peak.

Watch that silken coat
Fly straight
High in the air
To clear the gate.

Heading homeward
By and by,
But ask not when
Nor ponder why.

Aimless Amy

I smooth her silky dome-shaped head –
Those eyes intent upon my bread.
Shuffling rump and lolling tongue
Are we not strange to dwell among?

She loves the heat, she hates the rain –
Exists for food and shies from pain
But no art, speech or abstract thought,
Just pleasure when a ball is caught.

Denied her pack with whom to race,
An armchair is her favourite place.
She reads my face but does not blame me.
Poor old brainless,
Aimless
Amy.

Alsatian at the Station

I met an Alsatian at the station.
I had reservations as he stared at me in expectation.
I wondered at the inclination
Of this representation of the Alsatian nation.

Was his occupation participation
In a police operation in anticipation
Of some pilferation at this location,
Or was he just there on vacation?

In my imagination I sensed his salivation
And with slight regurgitation
In my nervous rumination,
I put my glasses on.

And what a revelation!

The Alsatian at the station
Was a plastic fabrication
With a slot for a donation!

Now had dawned realisation
Of my misinterpretation –
It was part hallucination!

First a calming relaxation was my primary sensation,
And in joyful celebration (and slight overcompensation)

I put one pound seventy-eight pence in!

But…
My jubilation turned to consternation when,
Not having a reservation,
I didn't have enough for a ticket
To my destination.

I'd been a victim of intimidation!
I felt irritation
Toward that imitation Alsatian at the station.

Why can't they just put an ordinary collection box out?

It's victimisation via Alsatian plasticization and exploitation of those in the population with a magnification limitation!

Bedlington

My Bedlington Terrier
Looks like a sheep,
So when I can't sleep
I count Bedlingtons.

Beware Dale of the Airdale!

Beware Dale of the Airdale!
Don't tickle him under there Dale.
He may have golden hair Dale
But he isn't always fair Dale.

You need to be aware Dale
When you fuss him in his lair Dale.
He is no teddy bear Dale –
He's a fan of underwear Dale!

Dale?

DALE?!

Bichon Frise

There is a woolly Bichon Frise
Half way down our row.
He nips the back wheel of my bike
When down the road I go.

I'm sure he waits all day for me
To crank back up the bank,
Then like a dodgem I will weave
To thwart his thoughtless prank.

Over pavements, under arches,
Through a hedge we go.
Down a tight back entry where the
Vapers like to go.

Thrashing past the corner shop
And on toward the park.
A tight loop round the roundabout
(But carefully 'cos it's dark).

Down and up the underpass
Where loafers shoot the breeze,
I think I've lost that flippin' dog,
That hairy Bichon Frise!

I see the welcome lights of home –
I jubilantly scoff,
But then he belts out from the bins
And bites my back lamp off!

Bingo the Dingo

There goes Bingo the Dingo –
He's no wallaby.
Speaking the Outback lingo –
He's a walkabout wannabe.

Poor old Bingo the Dingo –
Cocked up didn't he?
Australia's miles from London zoo!
He'll get there….

eventually.

Borzoi Ballet

Tottering, teetering, pipe-cleaner poise –
Bourgeoisie toys, the balletic Borzois.
Proud, perpendicular, noble of nose,
Like triumphal arches they strike a fine pose.

Thus is each hound in its fine fleece of silk.
'Tis rare to see great royal beasts of this ilk.
The Tsar and Tsarina were no more endowed
When it came to the drawing of gasps from a crowd.

Chinese Crested Powderpuff

I'll say no more –
The name's enough!

Chow Chow

I generally avoid Sigmund Freud,
But now I know he had a Chow
Called Jofi to assist in his therapy,
I bow to his bit of high-brow know-how
That would avow to the wow-factor of the Chow Chow.

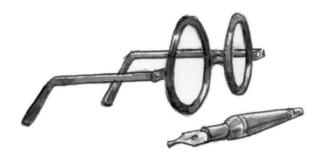

Cockerpoo

I could have had a Bogle,
A Bo-Jack or a Bugg,
A Rottsky, or a Rat-A-Pap,
A Cheagle or a Chugg.

I should have had A Labradane,
A Cojack or a Jug.
A Chorlie or a Doxiepoo,
A Foodle or a Frug.

I might have picked a Pekapoo,
A Bostie or a Bocker,
A Bowzer or a Baskimo,
A Shollie or a Shocker.

A Whoodle or a Schnoodle,
A Bichpoo or a Brat
But I plumped for a Cockerpoo –
I should have had a CAT!

Comedy Duo

A Boxer met a Bulldog –
They faced each other squarely.
The bulldog said that their proportions
Weren't apportioned fairly.

You are high and I am low,
I reach things very rarely
But looking at the snout department,
Both have been wrought sparely!

We grind our gormless under-bites,
With red eyes round and starey.
Kids don't rush to cuddle us,
Our dribbling makes them wary.

Humans like to laugh at us,
Our faces makes them jolly
And by the way my name is Stan,
Don't tell me… your's is Olly.

Dalmation Contemplation

I love a Dalmation but what drives me potty
Is when people get one and just call it Spotty!
Like giving your Granny a name such as Oldy
Or having a baby and calling it Baldy.

Get a Dalmation but don't call it Spotty,
Though I have to confess that I rather like Dotty.

Dandie Dinmont

Dandie Dinmont, I hear you say?
Is that a regency popinjay?
Is it an insect, a biscuit, a cake?
In terms of taxonomy it's a mistake!

Dogs don't have names as outrageous as that,
It's more what you'd call a ridiculous hat!
Could I say Dandie or rather just Dinmont –
Dan, maybe Din or possibly Danmont.

It sounds rather lunatic every which way,

But at least Dandie Dinmonts don't care what you say!

Dido

Here comes Dido down our lane,
She's the greatest of Great Danes.
Daft and dotty, tall and spotty,
Jumps the fence –
She's out again!

Look out!
Dido, likes to play –
Chasing kids around all day.
Long and lanky,
Slightly cranky.
Help!
NO DIDO!

GO AWAY!

Don't upset my Setter

Don't upset my Setter –
Just don't, you haven't met her.
She gets on so much better
With those who don't upset her.

You see, some folk don't get her,
They poke her and they pet her,
But she's an awful fretter –
She's a fusspot to the letter.

The vet, my friend Loretta
And a bloke in a bright red sweater,
Had cause to have regrets because
They did upset my Setter!

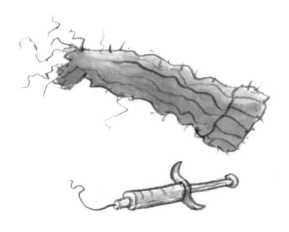

44

French Bulldog

My dog's got no nose –
He puffs and he blows.
He sneezes and wheezes
And hopes that it grows.

But he is a Bulldog
A les Français –
Conk not a prospect –
C'est non pour le nez!

Gypsy!

Gypsy! Not my sleeping bag!
Please get out of there!
And kindly disentangle yourself
From my underwear!

Don't scream like a fire alarm
When I go through the door.
Learn to cope when I go out –
Good sense we must restore!

Now settle down in your own bed,
Bonsoir ma petite chienne.
You are are my Enfant Terrible
            (Je n'regret rien).

Husky

I am a little Husky
(I've been howling too much).

Jack

Have you met my old dog Jack?
He's the leader of the pack.
Through the heathered hills we climb,
Even in the winter-time.

Jackie likes to travel far
But not inside a motor car.
He will cringe beneath a seat
And vomit breakfast on your feet.

So come with me and faithful Jack
But let's keep to the old straight track.
Modern transport can't be trusted –
Poor old Jackie's gut gets busted.

Komonder

Respect the woolly Komonder,
The shepherd of the flocks,
Making even sheep look sparse
With all those cool dreadlocks.

What a fluffy, funky pal,
You are to all those sheep,
Chasing wolves and bears away
So they can get to sleep!

Labrador

I love my Labrador …

Except when she snores
Or gnaws her paws
Or scores my floors
With her claws
Or roars when the postman
Knocks at the doors
Or stores old bones
In my drawers.

There's no applause
When she heaves
In hardware stores
But she's adored…

Most of the time,

Labradrawer

Lady Chihuahua

Lady Chihuahua
Reclined in her bower
Exerting her powers
On other bow-wowers.

Pheromones floating –
A female promoting.

Her tummy's slight bloating
Made Lady worth noting
To other dogs prowling.

She huffed at their howling
And sniffed at their fouling.
She pricked up her ears
To their masculine growling.

Lady Chihuahua –
In season – in flower.
Locked in her tower
She sensed her last hour.

She leapt through the letterbox,
Streaked down the stair,
Only to find
A GREAT DANE standing there!

Manchester Terrier

The Manchester Terrier
Unlike the city,
Is rather attractive
And some might say pretty.

Delicate, poised
And of two-tone design –
If Manchester looked as good
I would say,
Fine!

Mexican Hairless

The Mexican Hairless –
Was someone careless?
In the dim distant past
Was it caught in a blast?

I don't like to see a poor dog in a sweater
But in this case, I think it might look slightly better.

My Pug has a Bug

My Pug has a bug,
It has been there all day;
She rolls on the rug
But it won't go away!

She scritches and scratches
And claws at her ear.
It's deep in her lughole –
My goodness, oh dear!

My Pug had a bug,
But where has it gone?
She's chirpy again,
Is it over and done?

Is Puggie bug free?
Don't think she's not got 'em –
She's frantic again;
There's a wasp on her bottom!

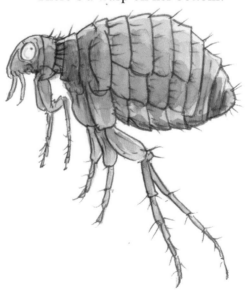

Neapolitan Mastiff

The Neapolitan Mastiff
Looks down and rather blue.
If you had a face that looked like that
Then you'd be cheesed off too!

Ode to Mongrels

I had a little mongrel,
I watched her body grow –
Was she this or was she that?
I didn't really know.

She grew waist-high with thick brown fur,
Her snout was long and mean.
Those teeth looked like the hunting kind
With edges sharp and keen.

Eventually my confusion
Reached its sorry end.
An expert on these things assured me,
'That's a Wolf my friend'.

Old English Sheep Dog!

The Old English Sheep Dog may advertise paint
But after a mud bath things don't look so quaint.

He's like a big mop that's been left to go foul –
He'll run with the hounds when he hears the pack howl.

Those twinkly blue eyes conceal chaos within –
Forget vinyl silk, he'll be raiding your bin.

Look out! Here he comes, lock the door, mind your
backs –
He'll kill for some contact, its love that he lacks!

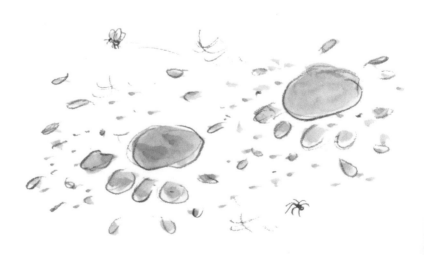

Oscar the Beagle

Oscar the Beagle won't go away,
He follows me down into town every day.
Oscar the Beagle joins all my trips,
He came to the seaside and ate half my chips.

Oscar the Beagle sits by my gate.
He bats not a lid when I tell him to wait.
Stay there! Don't follow me! Leave me alone!
Go and drink puddles or dig for a bone!

Oscar the Beagle stops for a pee
But I never quite lose him, he keeps hounding me.
And just when I think he has gone from my sight,
He's there up ahead with his nose shining bright.

Oscar the Beagle, you must let me be!
Please understand that I need to be free.
I don't want the sting of your tail on my thigh –
I don't care if you roll a big baleful eye.

Oh Oscar, please let me go solo, won't you?
This toilet compartment is not meant for two!
It's emotional black mail, that soppy-dog stare.
Oh, come on then, I'll just pretend you're not there.

Pedro

Here comes pretty Pedro
Wafting down the street.
Bitey, flighty Pedro –
He'll knock you off your feet.

Floaty fluffy Pedro –
He's not a meet and greet.
He'll hide out in a hedgerow
When he hears heavy feet.

Edgy, hedgy Pedro
Will never be your bud.
It's fight or flight with Pedro
You see, it's in his blood.

I'd love to sooth soft Pedro,
Just wrap my arms around
His leonine and hug-some face,
But Pedro's gone to ground.

Pointless

My Pointer won't point –
What can I do?
He won't point at me,
He won't point at you!

He won't point at anything
That Pointers should.
My Pointer is pointless
And that can't be good!

There's no point in Pointers
That won't point at owt.
To draw one's attention
Is what it's about!

If I am left wondering
When things pop out,
I'll miss opportunities –
There is no doubt!

Puggle

A Puggle likes to snuggle –
Happy huddle, cosy cuddle.
Yes, a puggle is a muggle,
Partly Pug and bits of Beagle
But it's not at all illegal,
You can get one with a struggle.

Don't be flummoxed and befuddled
Let me plug to you the Puggle!

Pyrenean
Mountain Dog

A Pyrenean Mountain Dog
                    Is not only a dog,
                              But also a

MOUNTAIN

To a
Yorshire Terrier.

Retriever Believer

I'm a believer in the Retriever
He fetches me this and he fetches me that.
It might be a sandal it might be a hat.
I suffer no losses if you want a stat'.

He's like a beaver, my eager Retriever,
Bringing back bits and fetching me bobs,
Things that get wobbly like wing nuts and knobs –
Yes, I'm a believer, he saves me some jobs!

He's not a diva, my humble Retriever –
He's like a cleaner I don't have to pay.
Socks don't get lost nor my underpants either –
Lord help me if ever my dog goes astray!

Saint Bernard

I took my big Saint Bernard
For a walk to town one day –
Before I travelled twenty feet
I heard some people say,
'Oh let us fuss that fluffy dog,
Oh let us feel that fur'.
She doesn't have a lot to do,
It's quite alright with her

But drawing such attention
makes our progress rather slack.
It's late when we get to the shops
And time we started back.
So if I get another dog,
I won't be such a wally,
I'll buy a tiny Pekingese
And hide it in my trolley!

Saluki

Salubrious Saluki,
Looking rather spooky.
Freaky,
Meekly cheeky,
Tall and creaky,
Beaky,
Sneaky.
Lofty,
Wafty,
Hairy,
Wary,
Taking off
If things get scary.
Slinky,
Slender,
Slightly crazy.
Looking haughty,
Naughty,
Dazy.
There are lots of single sentences
To sum up the Saluki
But if you want a single word,
You can't go wrong with
Kooky.

Samoyed

The Samoyeds keep you warm in bed,
So soft and snug they be.
They keep us Arctic children safe
When winds blow angrily.

There is no dread when the Samoyed
Curls round your frozen knees,
Nobody wants to wake up dead
In minus forty degrees.

While the Northern Lights flash in the night
We are safe inside our cot –
With a Samoyed next to your head
You can actually get too hot!

Schnauzer

A Schnauzer is the kind of dog
That I would like to be;
Handsome whiskers, jaunty brows
And under two foot three!

A Schnauzer is the kind of dog
That brightens up the home
And when he's on the lawn
Voila! An extra garden gnome!

Shar Pei

Shar Pei, Shar Pei
From old Hong Kong,
His coat is large,
His legs are strong.
His floppy face
looks slightly wrong
But that's the way
His genes have gone.

Shar Pei, Shar Pei
(Please play the gong)
His dynasty has lasted long,
But still his coat
Needs taking in –
Please pass me
That there safety pin.

Shih Tzu

My Shih Tzu
Belongs in a zoo
And as for the other bit –
I'm not going to mention it!

Staffie

My Staffie keeps me guessing,
I can't tell what mood he's in.
Sometimes he looks so happy
But he's miserable as sin.

He has a cheerful countenance,
His face is built for happy,
So when he's glum I'm guessing some –
Is he a happy chappy?

For sad or seething, shocked or shy
He shows his grinning choppers.
Those who misinterpreted
My Staffie have come croppers.

But do not fear, my Staffie dear
Is mostly feeling up –
He seldom sheds a solemn tear
(He was a cheerful pup).

Just tickle him behind the ear
That's what he loves the most.
But if you're cruel his golden rule
Is one chance and you're toast!

The Royal Corgis

HRH has a Corgi,
In fact she has a few –
They are her loyal subjects
(Yes folks, it is true).

They use the royal china,
They flop down where they like
And if Prince Philip shouts at them
The Queen says,
'On yer bike!'

The Skye Terrier Song
(To the tune of a well known Scottish melody)

Sing me a song of a land far away
Where a wee pooch ye'll see.
Low to the groond with his hair in his ee,
'Where is that dog?' they say.

Here he comes now, under a cow –
Down in a ditch all day.

Sing me a song of the doogie of Skye
Out on the moor is he.
Clarty wi' crud and tangled he be,
Pestered by ticks and flies.

Here he comes now, dew on his brow –
Softly he'll tip-toe by.

Sing me a song that's shorter than long,
Like the wee beast of Skye.

Thieving Hound

Arnold is a thieving hound
Whenever he gets out.
If the gate is left undone
He's off to gad about.

He heads straight for the washing lines,
And leaps high in the air
Till down he comes with tartan socks
(A Black Watch matching pair).

He'll tug at an elastic strap
Until a bra breaks free.
He'll rip a pair of knickers off
And not too carefully.

He's fond of frilly nighties
And those flimsy under-slips.
When he has gathered all he can
Back to HQ he nips.

Mum, whose are these boxer shorts
And these wide slacks ain't yours!
And I know for a fact that you
Don't wear such massive drawers!

Please don't make me take stuff back,
I do not get applause
When folk discover that their pants
Have been in Arnold's jaws!

Let's go to the jumble sale,
Donate some underwear
And let's go to the pet shop –
They buy any old dog there.

I don't care how we do it
This hound has gone too far.
I will not be seen handing back
Our next-door neighbour's bra!

Westie Bestie

A Westie is my bestie,
Has a cough, is rather chesty,
Stays in bed when I get dressed,
He won't be pressed to leave his nest.

He is my faithful friend, my Westie –
Can be awkward and a pestie
But he is a welcome guest,
He will forever be my Bestie.

Whippet

I said to my Whippet,
'Stop it!
Quit it!
Hop it!
Drop it!
Don't pop it!'

He bit it!

Wolfman

There is a hairy Wolfman
Who learned the wild wolf ways.
He disappears into the bush
And hangs out there for days.

He sleeps inside the wolf cave,
In the centre of the pack.
His wife has had enough,
She won't be there when he gets back.

Printed in Poland
by Amazon Fulfillment
Poland Sp. z o.o., Wrocław

54891065R00065